The Confidence Journal

A Journey Toward Self-Confidence

Enjoy the journey!
T Matheny

Tami Matheny

Dedication

"The Confidence Journal" is dedicated in loving memory of Walter Mathews. Walt was a special friend that came into my life at a time when I needed someone to remind me of my strengths, uniqueness, and the impact I could make. Despite the years and distance, he continued making a difference in my life. Unfortunately, in 2019 the world lost an amazing man, but Heaven gained another angel. Here's to you Walt!

We all need people like Walt in our lives to remind us of how special we are and what we have the potential to do. I've been blessed to have had more than my share of these people.

This book is also dedicated to each one of you taking the time to embark on this journey. It is you and ultimately you alone that determines your confidence. Here's to taking the first step!

The Idea Behind This Journal

Consistent confidence always eluded me. I was confident as long as I was performing well at whatever I was doing, and as long as I received the feedback I desired from others. But when these things didn't happen, I was on the confidence roller-coaster quickly. The ride wore me out. Finally, after a long journey, I got off the roller coaster and realized I alone, could control my confidence. In my book, "The Confident Athlete" I identified 4 areas that enable us to build and maintain our confidence. Since then I have added other areas that can influence our confidence. Get off the roller coaster and join me on one of the most rewarding journeys you will ever embark upon. For when you find consistent confidence, limits disappear, and the world is yours.

The theme for this journal follows the monthly calendar based off "The Confident Athlete".

April '19

The Confident Athlete:
4 Easy Steps to Build and Maintain Confidence

Start Strong Sunday	Make a Difference Monday	Talk the Talk Tuesday	Walk the Walk Wednesday	Thankful Thursday	Focused Friday	See it, Be it Saturday
Doing something seemingly small every day will lead you to something bigger.	1 April Fool's Day Impossible is a word to be found only in the dictionary of fools.	2 "Never say anything about yourself you do not want to come true" -Brian Tracy	3 Your mind and body are linked. Strong body language creates confidence.	4 National Vitamin C Day Will your attitude be a germ or a big dose of Vitamin C? -Jon Gordon	5 Focus on the present moment. It is the only one that matters.	6 A cause of success or failure is the image you have of yourself.
7 Read Today Reading the inspiring words of others can give you a confidence boost.	8 "One of the secrets of life is that all that is really worth the doing is what we do for others." -Lewis Carroll	9 Evaluate negative thoughts rationally. Respond with affirmations of what is good about you or the situation.	10 A smile is a deadly weapon against daily challenges and struggles	11 Today, be grateful that you have the ability to make difficult choices.	12 National Day of Silence Focus on really listening and hearing others.	13 A clear vision with a plan can provide a strong dose of confidence and power.
14 People often feel less confident about new or difficult situations. Planning & preparing for the unknown increases confidence.	15 For a boost of confidence, spread love and kindness to everyone you encounter today.	16 "Being negative only makes the journey more difficult. You may be given a cactus, but you don't have to sit on it." — Joyce Meyer	17 Acting as if you have confidence can actually help you build it.	18 Once you realize how valuable you are and how much you have going for you, life changes for the better.	19 Learn to view problems as possibilities that you haven't found an answer for yet.	20 Mental practice is almost as effective as physical. Doing both produces the greatest results.
21 Negative people bring others down. Surround yourself with positive, upbeat people.	22 Make a difference in someone's life. You then impact everyone influenced by them throughout their life.	23 National Take a Chance Day Confidence comes from taking action on your thoughts.	24 Practice self-care. Taking care of your body is a game changer.	25 Complaining creates more to complain about. Gratitude creates more to be grateful for.	26 When anxious, scared, etc. focus on your breathing. Breathe out the negative emotions. Inhale confidence.	27 "I never hit a shot, even in practice, without a sharp, in focus picture of it in my head." -Jack Nicklaus
28 Superhero Day Superheroes find allies & accept their support. Build your dream team today.	29 When you give back it makes everything more meaningful.	30 Our thoughts hold the power to everything in our lives.		"The Confident Athlete" is available online at Amazon & Barnes and Noble	26 Twitter: @taniinatheny @r2lcoaching Instagram: @refuse2losecoaching	

If you would like to receive April's Confidence Calendar go to www.r2lc.com and click on the link at the bottom

Make a Difference Monday's- when you strive to make a difference and give to others, it automatically increases your confidence.

Talk the Talk Tuesday's- your self-talk is a big factor in your confidence. Every time you speak to yourself, you are either increasing or decreasing your confidence.

Walk the Walk Wednesday's- How you carry yourself has a strong influence on your thoughts. Confidence can be generated by your body language.

Thankful Thursday's- an attitude of gratitude can change your focus and increase your confidence.

Focus Friday's- what you focus on grows. Learning to control your focus increases confidence.

See it Be it Saturday's- Confidence comes from seeing what you want. After all, seeing is believing.

Start Strong Sunday's- Preparation is the key to starting strong. Preparing our minds and bodies naturally increases confidence.

How to Use This Journal

Doing something seemingly small every day will lead you to something bigger. Confidence is similar to other physical skills. The more you work on it, the stronger you become.

Use this book as a journey toward confidence. The journal starts each day with a new daily confidence quote, tip or challenge. It is up to you how to use the space beneath it. Use it to write your thoughts, your confidence level that day, then finish with 3 things you were grateful for and 3 things that went well.

Or, use as a normal journal. Enjoy the daily message and use the rest of the page for your thoughts or notes at work or school.

This journal does not include dates so you can start it any time of the year.

**Confidence is the foundation
to all sustained success.**

Confidence is Key

Confidence is Key

When you make a difference and give to another, it automatically increases your confidence.

#MakeaDifference

Confidence is Key

Create and start using an "I am…" statement.
(i.e. "I am confident", "I am smart")

#TalktheTalk

Confidence is Key

**Stand in front of a mirror in a
Superman/Wonder Woman
Pose for 3 minutes.**

#WalktheWalk

Confidence is Key

Start each morning off by listing everything you are thankful for.

#Thankful

Confidence is Key

Focus on your strengths. Start by listing all that come to mind. Come back periodically and add to the list.

#Focus

Confidence is Key.

Start the day with a boost of confidence by spending 5-10 minutes seeing yourself as the confident person you wish to be.

#SeeitBeit

Confidence is Key

Confidence is a skill that needs consistent practice.

#Prepare

Confidence is Key

Find a social media post (Twitter, Facebook, Instagram, etc.) that inspires you.   Then share it with others.

#MakeaDifference

Confidence is Key

Talk to yourself as you would to your best friend.

#TalktheTalk

Confidence is Key

Focus on having strong body language throughout the day.

#WalktheWalk

Confidence is Key

**Text a friend, teammate, co-worker, etc.
and thank them for something specific.**

#Thankful

Confidence is Key

Focus on what is going right
vs. what is going wrong

#Focus

Confidence is Key

When we visualize, we have the power to see whatever we want without limitations. Start visualizing your dreams.

#SeeitBeit

Confidence is Key

Focus on Preparation:
Consistent Preparation leads
to Consistent Confidence.

#Prepare

Confidence is Key

Find and focus on other people's positives vs. their negatives.

#MakeaDifference

Confidence is Key

Get rid of "Don't". Your brain doesn't recognize the word "don't", so you still end up picturing whatever it is you said "don't" about.

#TalktheTalk

Confidence is Key

To break a negative thought, look to the sky or ceiling and hold your stare for 10 seconds.

#WalktheWalk

Confidence is Key

**Thank someone from your past that has
helped you get where you are today.**

#Thankful

Confidence is Key

Focus on past successes.

#Focus

Confidence is Key

Every night before going to sleep, see
yourself in detail having the game winner,
being successful at work, doing well on a
test or presentation, etc.

#SeeitBeit

Confidence is Key

This week make a plan that will prepare you mentally, physically, technically, and emotionally.

#Prepare

Confidence is Key

Today is a mindset. Put on your positive
pants and go make a difference.

#MakeaDifference

Confidence is Key

**Self-talk is the most powerful form
of communication. It either
propels you or pulls you back.**

#TalktheTalk

Confidence is Key

Body language doesn't talk; it screams.

#WalktheWalk

Confidence is Key

Write a thank you to yourself for the extra work you have put in this week.

#Thankful

Confidence is Key

Focus on what you can control.
Let go of what you can't.

#Focus

Confidence is Key

A tiger doesn't lose sleep over the opinion of sheep. What's important is how you see yourself, not how others do.

#SeeitBeit

Confidence is Key

One important key to success is self-confidence. An important key to self-confidence is preparation."
~Arthur Ashe

#Prepare

Confidence is Key

Today do something that makes a difference to your family, team, or community.

#MakeaDifference

Confidence is Key

"This is Good"

A story is told of an African king who had a close friend with whom he grew up. The friend had a habit of looking at every situation that occurred in his life (positive or negative) and remarking, "This is good!" Because of this, the king took his friend with him wherever he went.

One day the king and his friend were out on a hunting expedition. As they went along the friend would load and prepare the guns for the king. The friend had apparently done something wrong in preparing one of the guns, for after taking the gun from his friend, the king fired it and his thumb was blown off. Examining the situation, the friend remarked as usual, "This is good!" to which the king replied, "No, this is NOT good!" and angrily sent his friend to jail.

About a year later, the king was with his hunting party when they were captured by a band of cannibals. The cannibals began to kill and eat the hunting party one by one. However, when the cannibals got to the king, they realized he was missing a thumb. Being superstitious, they never ate anyone who was missing a body part and so, untying the king, they sent him on his way.

The king rushed to the jail where his friend was imprisoned and exclaimed, "You saved my life! Thank you, thank you". To which his friend replied, "This is good!".

"Yes, this is good for me, but I am sorry for sending you to jail" the king responded. *"No,"* his friend replied, *"This is good!"* *"What do you mean?"* asked the king. *"How is it good that I sent you to jail for a year?"* *"If I had NOT been in jail, I would have been with you and been eaten by the cannibals."* (Author unknown)

Find the "This is Good" in very situation.

#TalktheTalk

Shoulders back, head high, smile on!

#WalktheWalk

Confidence is Key

Show gratitude today by thanking someone that goes unnoticed (janitor, trainer, etc.).

#Thankful

Confidence is Key

Focus on the present moment.
It's the only one that matters.

#Focus

Confidence is Key

When you visualize, it adds an image to your self-talk.

#SeeitBeit

Confidence is Key

Start a success journal. List your successes at the end of each week. Make sure you include the adversity you overcame.

#Prepare

Confidence is Key

Successful, happy people look for ways to build confidence in others. What can you do today to build confidence in someone else?

#MakeaDifference

Confidence is Key

Change your self-talk by:
Recognizing it. Then reframing it so
its either positive and/or productive.

#TalktheTalk

Confidence is Key

Your body communicates as well as your mouth. Don't contradict yourself.

#WalktheWalk

Confidence is Key

Confidence, like gratitude, is a skill anyone can acquire but both require consistent practice.

#Thankful

Confidence is Key.

**Focus on what you can do
vs. what you can't do.**

#Focus

Confidence is Key

**Line the walls of your mind with pictures
of the confident, successful self
you wish to be.**

#SeeitBeit

Confidence is Key

Read a book on confidence.

#Prepare

Confidence is Key

Instill a positive belief in someone who needs to hear your encouraging words.

#MakeaDifference

Confidence is Key

"All that we are is the result of what we have thought. The mind is everything. What we think we become." – Buddha

#TalktheTalk

Confidence is Key

**For a confidence boost-
walk faster and more upright today.**

#WalktheWalk

Confidence is Key

Jot down things you are grateful for. Post them around your home.

#Thankful

Confidence is Key

Stop and take a moment to appreciate what you "get to do vs "have to do" today.

#Focus

Confidence is Key

"The secret of achievement is to hold a picture of the success outcome in mind" - **Henry David Thoreau**

#SeeitBeit

Confidence is Key

Don't waste the physical work by not putting in the mental work.

#Prepare

Confidence is Key

Be somebody that makes everyone feel like a somebody.

#MakeaDifference

Confidence is Key

**Instead of "oh no what if…"
tell yourself, "why not" and go for it.
Don't let fear hold you back.**

#TalktheTalk

Confidence is Key

Nodding can improve confidence in your thoughts. Its signals "yes, I can" to your brain.

#WalktheWalk

Confidence is Key

**Be thankful and loving of yourself today.
You are a gift.**

#Thankful

Confidence is Key

**Lack of confidence is often due to comparisons. Stop comparing.
Stay focused on you and your strengths.**

#Focus

Confidence is Key

Dreams are the first step, for they create a picture in our minds. Dream big today!

#SeeitBeit

Confidence is Key

The future depends on what you do today.

#Prepare

Confidence is Key.

Do something today that will raise your team/family/friends higher
We > Me

#MakeaDifference

Confidence is Key

Our lives move in the direction of our most dominant thoughts.

#TalktheTalk

Confidence is Key

Dress for Success. We tend to treat ourselves differently and more confidently when we are dressed in the right clothing for the moment.

#WalktheWalk

Confidence is Key

**List all the reasons you are thankful to play your sport/instrument, to have the job you have, or to be in school where you are.
Keep that list where you can see it.
Read it periodically.**

#Thankful

Confidence is Key

**Successful people show up how they
need to be vs. how they feel.**

#Focus

Confidence is Key

Create a vision board (collage/picture) of your vision or goals for the next year.

#SeeitBeit

Confidence is Key.

Confidence comes before competence.
Anchor your confidence to the
belief that you will get better with
practice. Then put in the practice.

#Prepare

Confidence is Key

Make a difference with yourself this week, by focusing on your health. Healthy minds and bodies are generally confidence bodies.

#MakeaDifference

Confidence is Key

**Health isn't just about what you're eating.
It's also about what you're thinking
and saying to yourself.**

#TalktheTalk

Confidence is Key

Stay strong by exercising regularly. Exercise releases endorphins. Endorphins fuel positivity and confidence.

#WalktheWalk

Confidence is Key.

Mental and physical health are strongly linked to the role gratitude plays in our lives'. It improves relationships, health, sleep, confidence, and satisfaction with life.

#Thankful

Confidence is Key

Focus on healthy relationships. Don't stay involved with anyone/anything that isn't aligned to your values. Healthy alignment builds a strong foundation of confidence.

#Focus

Confidence is Key

**Create a picture in your mind of the healthy,
confident, successful person you wish to be.**

#SeeitBeit

Confidence is Key

Taking care of your body improves confidence. Start by getting enough sleep, eating healthy, and staying hydrating.

#Prepare

Confidence is Key

Send an encourage note or text to someone that needs a pick me up today.

#MakeaDifference

Confidence is Key

Eliminate "enough's"
(i.e. "I am not pretty enough,"
or "I am not smart enough", etc.)

#TalktheTalk

Confidence is Key

Wear a Scent. Studies show when people wear perfume or cologne, it improves how they perceive themselves.

#WalktheWalk

Confidence is Key

Be thankful for your failures. They are often the biggest assets to success.

#Thankful

Confidence is Key

Every time you face a challenge or problem, focus on what you have the power to change.

#Focus

Confidence is Key

Imagine as you breathe in, you're breathing in confidence or focus. When exhaling imagine that you are breathing out fear, nerves or uncertainty.

#SeeitBeit

Confidence is Key

Take time to relax and rejuvenate yourself.
Balance in life is necessary for sustained
confidence and success.

#Prepare

Confidence is Key

Confidence is contagious. So is lack of...”
-Vince Lombardi. Be contagious today!

#MakeaDifference

Confidence is Key

The way you speak to yourself matters the most. It forms the narrative of your beliefs about yourself.

#TalktheTalk

Confidence is Key

For a confidence boost:
Imagine a rope pulling the top of your head
toward the sky, straightening
the rest of your body.

Confidence is Key

#WalktheWalk

Confidence is Key

Be thankful ahead of something happening,
plant seeds for it to happen. Show faith
And be thankful in advance.

#Thankful

Confidence is Key

Forward Focus!
Focus on the future. Your life
follows your thoughts. Only look
back to see how far you have come.

#Focus

Confidence is Key

Mental practice is almost as effective as physical practice. Doing both is more effective than either alone.

#SeeitBeit

Confidence is Key

After every test, project, competition, performance, etc., list 5 specific things you did well and 2 things you will do better next time.

#Prepare

Confidence is Key

Pay It Forward Today.

#MakeaDifference

Confidence is Key

Tell your negative self-talk, "Thanks for your input but I'm not interested".

#TalktheTalk

Confidence is Key

**Laughing increases endorphins,
which increase happiness and confidence.**

#WalktheWalk

Confidence is Key

Complaining attracts more things to complain about. Gratitude attracts more things to be thankful about.

#Thankful

Confidence is Key

Focus & Finish.
Don't let perfect get in the
way of being your best.

#Focus

Confidence is Key

Hang a photo on your mirror or refrigerator
of a time you felt confident. Look at it often.
Reflect on the steps it took to get there.

#SeeitBeit

Confidence is Key

Make a Confident Playlist.
Use songs that make you feel confident,
powerful, determined, etc.

#Prepare

Confidence is Key

"You aren't a true success unless you are helping others be successful"
-Jon Gordon

#MakeaDifference

Confidence is Key

Talking to yourself in 3rd person,
can have a greater impact on
motivation and confidence.

#TalktheTalk

Confidence is Key

As you act, so you become. As you change
your body language, so you become.

#WalktheWalk

Confidence is Key

Be grateful of where you are today.
You are there for a reason.

#Thankful

Confidence is Key

What you focus on grows.

#Focus

Confidence is Key

**What we see often depends on
what we look for.**

#SeeitBeit

Confidence is Key

"If you fail to prepare, you're prepared to fail." – **Mark Spitz**

#Prepare

Confidence is Key

Make a difference in your own life,
by not making excuses.
Take responsibility instead.

#MakeaDifference

Confidence is Key

**Toss away the "could have's"
and "should have's".**

#TalktheTalk

Confidence is Key

Deep breathing is a simple skill that can calm your body and boost your confidence.

#WalktheWalk

Confidence is Key

**Talk more about your blessings
than your burdens.**

#Thankful

Confidence is Key

Lasting confidence doesn't come from your past nor outside factors. It comes from the inside out.

#Focus

Confidence is Key

See ahead of time what you want to happen. Michael Jordan always took the last shot in his mind BEFORE playing.

#SeeitBeit

Confidence is Key.

**Prepare ahead. Know in advance how
you will handle any situation thrown at you.**

#Prepare

Confidence is Key

Drop, avoid, or ignore those that bring you down. Surround yourself with positive people.

#MakeaDifference

Confidence is Key

"Success is a tale of obstacles overcome, and for every obstacle overcome, an excuse not used." ~Robert Brault

#TalktheTalk

Confidence is Key

Wearing costumes give us power to be free to act a role. Why not wear your confidence costume every day of the year!

#WalktheWalk

Confidence is Key

Gratitude makes sense of our past, brings peace for today, and creates a vision for tomorrow. ~ Melody Beattie

#Thankful

Confidence is Key

What to do with a mistake- recognize it, admit it, learn from it, forget it" -Dean Smith

#Focus

Confidence is Key

228

Imagining yourself doing specific tasks in detail, helps you improve them. Practice this 5-10 min a day.

#SeeitBeit

Confidence is Key

**Find a confidence quote that inspires you.
Write it down and post in places where
you will see it often.**

#Prepare

Confidence is Key

A smile is a tiny thing that can make big difference in not only others, but also, in you.

#MakeaDifference

Confidence is Key

If you realized how powerful your thoughts were, you would never think another negative thought again.

#TalktheTalk

Confidence is Key.

Smile even if fake at first. Studies show that a fake smile is often enough to turn a bad day into a good one.

#WalktheWalk

Confidence is Key

Be thankful today that you and you alone get to choose to be confident or not.

#Thankful

Confidence is Key

Kaizen: small, continuous, daily improvement. What can you do 1% better today?

#Focus

Confidence is Key

We aren't limited by what our eyes can
or can't see, but by what our
mind can or can't see.

Confidence is Key

#SeeitBeit

Confidence is Key

244

**Confidence starts with preparation.
Prepare by focusing on 1st things 1st.**

#Prepare

Confidence is Key

Celebrate someone else's success today.

#MakeaDifference

Confidence is Key.

Get in the habit of telling yourself what you want to happen vs. what you are scared will happen.

Confidence is Key

#TalktheTalk

Confidence is Key

Confidence is showing up in every single moment like you're meant to be there.

#WalktheWalk

Confidence is Key

Entitlement works against gratitude.
Fight it by thanking people as they
give to you or help you.

#Thankful

Confidence is Key

Be where your feet are.

#Focus

Confidence is Key

For a boost of confidence, recall moments that have made you smile as well as moments that made you feel confident.

#SeeitBeit

Confidence is Key

Confidence is built, not birthed. If you want to be confident you have to work at it.

#Prepare

Confidence is Key

Confidence is Key.

Confidence is Key

What Now

*Use social media to build confidence.

*Follow "The Confident Athlete" on twitter @tamimatheny

*Subscribe to our Monthly Confidence Calendar. Go to www.r2lc.com and subscribe at the bottom of the page.

April '19

The Confident Athlete: 4 Easy Steps to Build and Maintain Confidence

Start Strong Sunday	Make a Difference Monday	Talk the Talk Tuesday	Walk the Walk Wednesday	Thankful Thursday	Focused Friday	See it, Be it Saturday
Doing something seemingly small every day will lead you to something bigger.	1 **April Fool's Day** Impossible is a word to be found only in the dictionary of fools.	2 "Never say anything about yourself you do not want to come true" -Brain Tracy	3 Your mind and body are linked. Strong body language creates confidence.	4 **National Vitamin C Day** Will your attitude be a germ or a big dose of Vitamin C? -Jon Gordon	5 Focus on the present moment. It is the only one that matters.	6 A cause of success or failure is the image you have of yourself.
7 **Read Today** Reading the inspiring words of others can give you a confidence boost.	8 "One of the secrets of life is that all that is really worth the doing is what we do for others." -Lewis Carroll	9 Evaluate negative thoughts rationally. Respond with affirmations of what is good about you or the situation.	10 A smile is a deadly weapon against daily challenges and struggles	11 Today, be grateful that you have the ability to make difficult choices.	12 **National Day of Silence** Focus on really listening and hearing others.	13 A clear vision with a plan can provide a strong dose of confidence and power.
14 People often feel less confident about new or difficult situations. Planning & preparing for the unknown increases confidence.	15 For a boost of confidence, spread love and kindness to everyone you encounter today.	16 "Being negative only makes the journey more difficult. You may be given a cactus, but you don't have to sit on it." – Joyce Meyer	17 Acting as if you have confidence can actually help you build it.	18 Once you realize how valuable you are and how much you have going for you, life changes for the better.	19 Learn to view problems as possibilities that you haven't found an answer for yet.	20 Mental practice is almost as effective as physical. Doing both produces the greatest results.
21 Negative people bring others down. Surround yourself with positive, upbeat people.	22 Make a difference in someone's life. You then impact everyone influenced by them throughout their life.	23 **National Take a Chance Day** Confidence comes from taking action on your thoughts.	24 Practice self-care. Taking care of your body is a game changer.	25 Complaining creates more to complain about. Gratitude creates more to be grateful for.	26 When anxious, scared, etc. focus on your breathing. Breathe out the negative emotions. Inhale confidence.	27 "I never hit a shot, even in practice, without a sharp, in focus picture of it in my head." -Jack Nicklaus
28 **Superhero Day** Superheroes find allies & accept their support. Build your dream team today.	29 When you give back it makes everything more meaningful.	30 Our thoughts hold the power to everything in our lives.		"The Confident Athlete" is available online at Amazon & Barnes and Noble	Twitter: @tamimatheny @r2lcoaching Instagram: @refuse2losecoaching	

If you would like to receive April's Confidence Calendar go to www.r2lc.com and click on the link at the bottom

*Read "The Confident Athlete: 4 Easy Steps to Build and Maintain Confidence." This book isn't just for athletes. It provides strategies for anyone looking to build and maintain confidence.

Other Books by Tami Matheny

"This is Good: A Journey on Overcoming Adversity"

Adversity is often seen as a bad thing. Something to avoid. But to accomplish anything worthwhile adversity is necessary. It is what separates the great from the mediocre, the champions from the contenders. The difference is in how you look at adversity. Success comes from learning to see it, think about it, and respond to it in a positive or productive way. Creating a "this is good" mindset will allow you to do this. This is a story within a story. It is how an African folk lore transformed a college soccer team to reach heights they didn't know they could. You will follow their journey and the lessons along the way that enable them to cultivate a new way of thinking.

"The Confident Athlete: 4 Easy Steps to Build and Maintain Confidence"

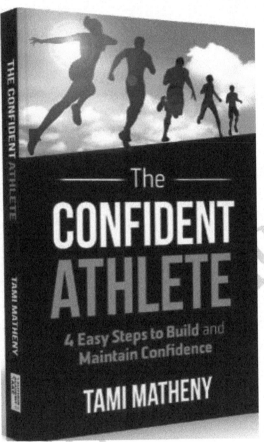

"The Confident Athlete" is not just for athletes. It provides strategies for anyone looking to build and maintain confidence. Matheny gives 4 basic building blocks to ensure you start and end each performance with a tank full of confidence. Coaches, athletes, teams, parents, and even non-athletes will discover simple yet powerful ways to build and maintain confidence. The book will give you the tools to be able to maintain confidence in the face of adversity. Confidence is a skill that can be cultivated through repetitions. Are you ready to take responsibility for your confidence and ensure that your confidence stays consistent?

Both are available on Amazon.
Contact tami@r2lc.com for group pricing.

Confidence is Key

Made in USA - Kendallville, IN
1238205_9781793370877
02.23.2021 0850